Honor the Diamond

Developing True Character
from Within

Brian Altenbach

Praise for *Honor the Diamond*

"Brian's compassion for the youth of today and love for baseball are displayed every time he steps onto the diamond."
—Mike Long, parent, coach, and umpire

"This very insightful book highlights the importance of character through real-life examples. It will absolutely inspire a young child as well as any parent to cultivate character to make a positive difference in the world. As a coach in the Babe Ruth League, I believe this book is a must-read for any player and parent."
—Anthony Vitale, DC, parent and chiropractor

"In reading, *Honor the Diamond*, I saw an instinctive ability of the Speech Ump to bring out the best in young people, by guiding them when they needed it most to dig deep within themselves to overcome the challenges that confronted them. He launches them successfully through their difficulties and into their life's journey with confidence. *Honor the Diamond* truly delivers its message: the development of true character. It's a potent, inspiring read for any age."
—Ron L Glazier, USMC Veteran

"Baseball has always been a game that teaches life lessons, but today's game has gotten away from teaching them. This book is a must-read on how parents, coaches, players, and umpires should approach the game and its value in teaching the players of today. The person you are is more important than the game being played."
—Eric Vernon, Cal Ripken coach and parent

Printed in the United States of America
Published in Hellertown, PA

Cover design by Tristan Altenbach

Library of Congress Control Number 2024904813
ISBN 978-1-958711-49-1

For more information or to place bulk orders, contact the author or the publisher at Jennifer@BrightCommunications.net.

Bright
COMMUNICATIONS

To the Cal Ripken League of the Lehigh Valley umpires, coaches, families, and players who have affectionately dubbed me the "Speech Ump." Their willingness to embrace my saying at the beginning of the games while endorsing the need for more character development with children was a major motivation in creating the book.

Contents

The Pre-Game: Play Ball!   10

The First Inning: Courage   13
Top of the First: Hit by Pitch   14
Bottom of the First: To Tell or Not to Tell   16

The Second Inning: Compassion   19
Top of the Second: Have Some Fun   20
Bottom of the Second: Miracle League   21

The Third Inning: Gratitude   23
Top of the Third: First Hit   24
Bottom of the Third: Pay It Forward   26

The Fourth Inning: Humbleness   29
Top of the Fourth: Caught Stealing   30
Bottom of the Fourth: It's a Compliment   32

The Fifth Inning: Honesty   35

Top of the Fifth: Blind Tag   36

Fifth Inning Stretch   38

Bottom of the Fifth: Ball on the Dresser   39

The Sixth Inning: Faith   43

Top of the Sixth: Throwing a Fit   44

Bottom of the Sixth: Grandfather   46

The Post-Game: Honor the Diamond   48

Acknowledgments   51

About the Author   53

The Pre-Game: Play Ball!

The start of another baseball season is upon us. It is a sunny spring evening as I am arriving to the game as the umpire. The rear hatch of the car is open as I am strapping on my umpiring gear for the competition. While preparing for the game, I can't help but think about one umpire I had growing up. We all knew him as Cobby. He was a portly, grey-haired man with a friendly smile and a great connection with everyone. No matter who won the game, Cobby was able to make every game he umpired enjoyable. It is my hope to bring the same joy and fun when I umpire.

The teams are on the field preparing for their competition. They are doing infield and outfield practice. They are taking fly balls and ground balls, throwing to the right base. Pitchers are throwing their warm-up pitches with the coaches. All are working to make few mistakes and planning to win the game. Meanwhile, some families are at the snack stand grabbing food. Other families are getting to their seats along their team's side of the field. Finally, I am dressed and begin my trek to the field. Some of the players recognize me, and the following can be heard:

"Hey, you're the speech ump. Are you giving that speech again?"

"Awesome, we like you, ump. You're a fun ump."

"We like when you ump our games!"

"I hope you're our ump today. You are my favorite ump."

While smiling to the players, I reply, "Have fun and do your best."

The plate meeting with the coaches is complete, and they join their players, who are already lined up on the foul line. The Pledge of Allegiance is recited by all. The players and coaches are asked to remain on the foul line for my customary saying:

"Gentlemen, Your character is more important than how good you are at any sport. Athleticism is temporary. Your character, the type of man you are, will last forever. Be compassionate, be grateful, be humble, be honest. Gentlemen, play ball!" (Author of this statement is unknown)

Photograph by Tyler Keifer

Bill Gold Field: Nazareth, Pennsylvania

The First Inning: Courage

cour • age

[/kerij/ • *noun*

The quality or mind of spirit that enables a person to face difficulty, danger, pain, etc.

The Baseball Scorecard

Notes:				Start Time:		Attendance:	
☐ Visitor:		Date:		End Time:		Wind:	
☐ Home:		Scorer:		Time of Game:		Weather:	

#	Line Up	Pos	1	2	3	4	5	6	7	8	9	10	AB	R	H	RBI

S	Runs										
U	Hits										
M	Errors										
S	Left on Base										

#	Pitchers	W/L/S	IP	H	R	ER	BB	SO	HB	BK	WP	TBF

#	Catchers	PB		Umpires	
				HP:	3B:
				1B:	
				2B:	

Top of the First: Hit by Pitch (Courage on the Field)

Dressed as the umpire for today's game, I entered the field and looked at all the players practicing and getting ready for the game. As the coaches were hitting fly balls to the fielders, one player caught my eye. He was bending over, covering his face with his right arm and holding his glove up in the air, hoping he wouldn't get hit by the ball. He took a quick peek and then hid his face again. The ball dropped, and he picked it up and threw it to the coach. Even as he took practice swings with a soft toss drill, he was tiptoeing and dancing in place, trying to avoid being hit by the baseball. I could hear the coach encouraging him every step of the way.

The game began, and the team moved through the batting order. The timid young boy I saw as I was walking onto the field finally came up to bat. Some tears were in his eyes as he stepped in and out of the batter's box. His eyes were wide open while his lips were quivering a little. I heard the coach yell encouragement, "Trevor, stay in there. You can do it." The pitch was over the plate as Trevor was jumping out of the box. Again I could hear the coach yell, "Stay in the box. You can do it!" The next pitch came in, and despite Trevor jumping out of the box, the ball hit him in the hip. Trevor started to cry and looked like he was trying to decide whether he wanted to get up or go to the dugout. When he finally decided to take his base, the coaches and his teammates encouraged him.

Later in the game, Trevor came up to bat again, with his walk slower, lips trembling faster, and eyes even wider, clearly showing his fear. I could see the conflict inside of Trevor, *Do I step in the batter's box or do I walk away?* I called "time out" and spoke to him, pointing to the area just below his heart, "Trevor, it takes courage to come back to the plate and bat again. I can tell there is a part of you that wants to do well. There are many other kids who won't even play. You have the courage to come and play. I believe deep inside of you, you can trust yourself and be able to get back and bat."

"I'm scared," Trevor said.

"Trevor, it's okay to be scared. Courage is using the feeling, deep inside of you wanting to do well, and facing that fear, no matter what happens. You can do it. Trust yourself."

Trevor took a deep breath, exhaled, and stepped into the batter's box. The first pitch almost hit him. Trevor looked at me with wide eyes as he jumped out of the way. I nodded to indicate I believed he could do it. There was a new look on Trevor's face as he stepped back into the box. He decided to take a swing and got a hit. He eventually came around the bases to score the winning run. Trevor was excited and smiling. After the game, he came over and thanked me for the encouragement.

I told Trevor, "Courage is being able to look at fear and use the strength deep inside you to face it, knowing you can do your best no matter the result."

We high-fived each other as we left the field.

Bottom of the First: To Tell or Not to Tell (Courage in Life)

The first game of the new season was on a warm, pleasant spring evening, and it was a refreshing feeling to get back on the field and start umpiring again. As I stood in the parking lot by my car and put on the umpiring gear, a ball player ran to get up to the field, looking rushed and frustrated. Before he ran past me, he stopped and looked at me.

"Hey, you're the speech ump! How are you doing? Do you remember me?" he asked excitedly.

I looked up from tying my shoes at the player, seeing a young man with a confident look on his face. "Hey, Trevor! Look at you! There's something different about you. How are you doing?"

"I'm doing fine," Trevor said. "I'm excited to be back playing again. Even though I was hit a couple times after our talk last year, I remembered what you said and kept trusting myself in what I wanted to do."

"That's awesome. I'm glad you kept trying. Stay strong and keep trusting yourself," I replied.

Trevor went on to say, "You know I was thinking about what you said last year about courage when a friend of mine told me about his father's drinking and beating he received. I was confused and didn't know what to do. He shared how he hates his dad's drinking and showed me some of the bruises his dad had left on him. I was afraid to say anything and didn't want him to get hurt even more. But I wanted to help."

"I hope he is okay," I stated.

"Well, I wasn't sure if I should say anything to anyone because I was afraid he was going to hate me and not be friends anymore. I felt myself shaking the way I did in the game last year, and then I remembered you pointing to my heart and telling me to trust myself."

"What did you do?" I asked.

"I decided to speak with the guidance counselor at school and share with her what my friend told me about his dad's drinking and the beatings he was getting," Trevor said with a big smile on his face.

I noticed his grin and asked, "Trevor, what are you smiling about?"

"After I shared the news with the guidance counselor, my friend came back and told me she spoke with him, and the family is getting help. The drinking and beatings have stopped, and his father started to apologize for his actions."

"Trevor, I'm proud of you. That took a lot of courage, and I'm glad you stood up for your friend."

"Yeah, me too! We're having a sleepover this Friday," Trevor said with excitement. "Thank you for encouraging me to trust myself."

"You're welcome, Trevor! Now let's go and have us some fun."

Photograph by Mike Laclair

Bangor Memorial Park Field: Bangor, Pennsylvania

The Second Inning: Compassion

com • pas • sion

/kəm 'paSH(ə)n/ • *noun*

A feeling of deep sympathy and sorrow for another along with the desire to ease the suffering

The Baseball Scorecard

Notes:				Start Time:		Attendance:	
☐ Visitor:		Date:		End Time:		Wind:	
☐ Home:		Scorer:		Time of Game:		Weather:	

#	Line Up	Pos	1	2	3	4	5	6	7	8	9	10	AB	R	H	RBI

S U M S												
	Runs											
	Hits											
	Errors											
	Left on Base											

#	Pitchers	W/L/S	IP	H	R	ER	BB	SO	HB	BK	WP	TBF

#	Catchers	PB	Umpires		
			HP:		3B:
			1B:		
			2B:		

Top of the Second: Have Some Fun (Compassion on the Field)

It was about the third inning in a close league game in a new season. There was one out, and all of the bases were empty. The batter who was up was a newer player, noticeably scared. The first pitch was inside, close to the batter, and his eyes were opened wide. The next pitch was a good speed and caught the batter square in the helmet, right near his ear.

After the coaches made sure the batter was okay, he started to walk to first. As the umpire, I was walking next to the batter when Sebastian, the pitcher, came over to walk with us and said, "I'm sorry. I hope you are okay. Be ready to run and have fun. You never know what might happen." Then Sebastian gave the batter a handshake and a wink.

The next two pitches were wild and in the dirt, allowing the runner to get to the next bag and then third base. The next batter got a hit with the run, scoring. Sebastian then struck out the next two batters to end the inning.

After the outs, I spoke to Sebastian. "I like how you encouraged the batter you hit to have fun and be ready to run. You threw those pitches in the dirt on purpose, didn't you?"

"I sure did," Sebastian said with a wry smirk on his face. "I wanted him to enjoy the game as well. Did you see the smile on his face?"

"I saw that smile," I said, pointing to Sebastian's heart. "Thank you for being a kind young man. It's so nice that you have such care for others. Please keep that up in all parts of your life."

Bottom of the Second: Miracle League (Compassion in Life)

Just a week later, I was in the parking lot of a local store and heard a voice call, "Hey, blue!"

I turned and asked, "Hey, Sebastian, how are you doing? It looks like you're going to a game."

"I'm doing okay. Well, I am going to a game, but it is a different game than the league I'm in. I was in trouble for picking on my brother the other day, and my parents grounded me. While I was grounded, I cleaned up my room. The business card you gave with the speech on it fell out of my baseball pants. Something inside of me made me think of our talk. I decided to donate time and work with kids in the Miracle League. So I am dressed and ready to play with them."

The Miracle League is a place where kids with physical challenges are paired up with other children to play baseball.

"You know," Sebastian continued, "making friends and giving these kids a chance to enjoy playing and be a part of a team allows me to realize how special life is. I want everyone to experience this type of joy. Even my brother."

"Sebastian, that is so awesome you are giving of your time in that way," I said.

"I'm glad you encouraged me to do this in all aspects of life," Sebastian said. "I'm reminded of the smile on the kid from our game, and I get to see those same excited smiles with the Miracle League every time I spend time with them."

"Sebastian, keep that big heart of yours! It's great to see the compassion you share for others. Have a great day," I said.

Photograph by Brian Altenbach

Lower Nazareth Township Park Field #2: Lower
Nazareth, Pennsylvania

The Third Inning: Gratitude

grat • i • tude

/ˈgradə tood/ • *noun*

Warmly and deeply expressing an appreciation of kindness or benefits received from another

The Baseball Scorecard

Notes:					Start Time:		Attendance:	
Visitor:		Date:			End Time:		Wind:	
Home:		Scorer:			Time of Game:		Weather:	

#	Line Up	Pos	1	2	3	4	5	6	7	8	9	10	AB	R	H	RBI

S U M S										
	Runs									
	Hits									
	Errors									
	Left on Base									

#	Pitchers	W/L/S	IP	H	R	ER	BB	SO	HB	BK	WP	TBF

#	Catchers	PB	Umpires	
			HP:	3B:
			1B:	
			2B:	

Top of the Third: First Hit (Gratitude on the Field)

It was getting late in the season, and the teams were about to play their final game. I noticed a particular player named Greyson trying his best to get a hit throughout different games that I had umped. At the beginning of the game, I asked the coach if Greyson had gotten his first hit. The coach indicated he was close a couple of times but was still looking for his first hit.

In the last inning of the game, Greyson came up to bat, still looking for his first hit.

The first pitch was a nice toss down the middle of the plate for the first strike of the at bat. The second pitch was a little high, and Greyson motioned as if he was going to swing and stopped for the first called ball. The third pitch was in the same spot without a swing, allowing for a second called ball. At the fourth pitch, he took a swing and just got a little bit of the ball. It was a slow grounder down the third base line with a spin on the ball. I could hear the collective gasp of the crowd. The ball was slowly moving down the line as I was following it to see if it stayed fair or went foul. The ball was spinning and slowly started to cross the foul line. The third baseman finally touched the ball.

"FOUL BALL," I yelled.

Greyson was able to foul off a couple of pitches. On the next pitch, he was able to make good contact and hit the ball between the third baseman and the shortstop. He ran as fast as he could and was finally able to stand on first base. The fans and crowd cheered loudly as he jumped up and down on first base, giving the coach a high five. He had gotten his first hit of the season—his first hit ever.

The pitcher struck out the last batter. As the teams lined up at the end of the game to shake hands, the opposing pitcher asked me if he could have the game ball.

"Sure," I said, guessing what he had in mind.

As the teams shook hands, the pitcher gave Greyson the game ball. "It's important to have the ball of your first hit," the pitcher said.

Greyson looked like he was in shock, with a great big smile upon his face. Both teams joined in a circle, and as I took Greyson's hand and held it in the air, everyone yelled, "Greyson, Greyson, Greyson!"

He had the biggest smile on his face and said, "Thank you. It means a lot to have your support. I'm grateful to have great players to cheer me on."

Bottom of the Third: Pay It Forward (Grateful in Life)

Several years had passed, and the current baseball season had ended. It was nearing the holidays. One day, I was walking to the grocery store, lost in thought. As I neared the entrance, I heard a deep voice yelling at me from the entrance, "Hey, blue, is that you? Aren't you that speech ump?"

As I turned to look, the face seemed familiar, but I was uncertain. I replied, "Yes, it's me. Forgive me: Your face looks familiar, but I forget your name."

"It's me, Greyson," he exclaimed. "You were chanting my name after I got my first hit of the season."

In shock, I said, "Greyson, it's you. It has been several years. How are you doing?"

"I'm a senior in high school, going into the Marines," he said. Then Greyson explained that he was just shopping for his family. In the checkout line, he was talking with a Vietnam veteran who is a Marine and asked when Greyson was joining, having seen his Marines Poolee shirt.

"While shopping and talking with the Marine veteran, I remembered when you got people cheering my name when the pitcher gave me the ball for my first hit," Greyson said. "It dawned on me that I wanted to show my gratitude to this veteran. I know how many Vietnam veterans were shunned and looked down upon after the war. I used some of the money my family gave me to pay for the Marine's groceries. I told him that I wanted to personally thank him for his sacrifice and dedication to our country and to show how grateful someone from my generation can be for that service. I actually wanted to thank you, blue, for the little cheer for my first hit. It was a great memory, and I wanted to pass it along."

"Greyson," I said, "I appreciate your demonstration of gratitude for the veteran. Best of luck in your endeavors as you offer your service. I'm glad that I was able to leave a lasting impression with a simple cheer."

We shook hands, smiling. As we took a couple steps backward, at the same time, we both placed our right hands over our hearts, symbolizing our gratitude and thankfulness for each other.

Photograph by Eric Vernon

Freemansburg Township Athletic Association:
Freemansburg, Pennsylvania

The Fourth Inning: Humbleness

hum • ble • ness

/ˈhəmb(ə)l/ • *adjective*

Having the feeling of being modest

The Baseball Scorecard

Notes:		Start Time:	Attendance:
☐ Visitor:	Date:	End Time:	Wind:
☐ Home:	Scorer:	Time of Game:	Weather:

#	Line Up	Pos	1	2	3	4	5	6	7	8	9	10	AB	R	H	RBI

S U M S												
	Runs											
	Hits											
	Errors											
	Left on Base											

#	Pitchers	W/L/S	IP	H	R	ER	BB	SO	HB	BK	WP	TBF

#	Catchers	PB

Umpires	
HP:	3B:
1B:	
2B:	

Top of the Fourth: Caught Stealing (Humbleness on the Field)

Here we were in another season of baseball. I was umpiring a game for twelve-year-olds, where leading and stealing bases are permitted. During this particular game, a right-hand pitcher had a man on first. The runner, Evan, started off toward second base as the pitcher was lifting his leg. The pitcher turned toward second and ran after Evan.

"Balk, that's a balk," yelled the runner, his face wrinkled in frustration as he jumped up and down. "It's a balk! I know it's a balk!"

The base umpire looked my way, confused, and shrugged his shoulders to suggest he was not sure what to call. After taking some time to consider the play, I finally made a call. I pointed to the runner, made a fist in the air, and yelled, "Out!"

Evan continued to complain, insisting it was a balk. As it was the third out, I took time to speak with Evan and the coach, who was also Evan's father, at the end of the inning.

"I might be confusing different sets of rules from the different leagues I ump," I said to them both. "I might have made a mistake. I will research and let both of you know.

"However, as a runner who is convinced in being right on a rule, you still have a job to get to the base," I said to Evan, pointing to his heart. "What would have happened with the rule if you had gotten to the base and been called safe?"

"The question about the rule would not have mattered because I'd have been safe," Evan said.

The game ended without any other rules being questioned. As soon as I got home, I reviewed the rules for the different leagues and found that Evan was correct for this league. I contacted the coach.

"Coach, I wanted to let you know I researched the rule, and your son was right. Let him know that I apologize for applying the wrong rule for the league."

"I was able to tell him right away," the coach said. "He admitted he was wrong for not completing his job and trying to get to the bag safely."

About a month later, at a local tournament, Evan's mother approached me and stated, "Thank you for what you did in admitting the mistake and letting my son know it happened. You made an impression on him. As parents, we truly appreciate your humbleness in admitting the mistake."

"Thank you," I replied. "I want to make sure we are teaching the kids good character traits."

Bottom of the Fourth: It's a Compliment (Humbleness in Life)

Later in the season, I was umpiring for the weekend fall tournament. In between games, Evan recognized me and came over to speak with me for a little. We spent some time talking about the call earlier in the season. We both laughed at the mistake, and Evan said he appreciated my letting him know about my mistake. After we laughed for a time, there were some small discussions about getting back into the swing of school. Just as we were chilling, eating hot dogs, and drinking soda, Evan asked if I minded if he shared something with me.

He told me about a school group project he was working on. Evan said he had taken on the more involved task, and some of his friends had often complimented him on his work. He mentioned his response was typically, "It's no big deal."

As these exchanges continued, his friends began to express their frustration, feeling like he was minimizing and blowing off their compliments. The tension grew because the project seemed to be getting tougher as it went along. Because Evan believed he was just doing his job, he became confused at his friends' reactions. He reflected upon our interaction, and he wondered if people should be humble in accepting compliments.

He started to accept his friends' compliments by saying, "Thank you. I appreciate it." Although that felt odd to Evan at first, his friends seemed to be happier, and they also wanted to help out more with the project. Next thing Evan knew, the group joined together to complete the project a week before it was due, and they got an A.

After Evan shared that story with me, he said, "Being humble is being able to be gracious with compliments and criticisms while remaining true to yourself as a person."

"Thank you for sharing, Evan. Stay humble," I said with a hand over my heart.

Photograph by Steve Solderich

Bushkill Township Recreational Fields, Field #10:
Nazareth, Pennsylvania

The Fifth Inning: Honesty

hon • es • ty

/'änᵊstē/ • *noun*

Showing uprightness and fairness, being truthful, ethical, and fair

The Baseball Scorecard

Notes:						Start Time:			Attendance:					
Visitor:			Date:			End Time:			Wind:					
Home:			Scorer:			Time of Game:			Weather:					

#	Line Up	Pos	1	2	3	4	5	6	7	8	9	10	AB	R	H	RBI

S	Runs									
U	Hits									
M	Errors									
S	Left on Base									

#	Pitchers	W/L/S	IP	H	R	ER	BB	SO	HB	BK	WP	TBF

#	Catchers	PB	Umpires	
			HP:	3B:
			1B:	
			2B:	

Top of the Fifth: Blind Tag (Honesty on the Field)

A local Pennsylvania community holds an annual tournament for Father's Day weekend. This is a chance to umpire different games, working with kids of different ages, while meeting different people. Typically, some play or scenario makes the weekend unique. A nine-year-olds' game I was umpiring by myself offered one of those moments.

In one inning, there was a runner on first. The hitter had a drive toward the second baseman, close to second base. As I moved to see if the second baseman was tagging the runner, the pitcher stood and moved to block my view of the play. There was a motion to try to tag the runner, but I did not have a clear view of what occurred. I initially called the runner safe, then called time-out and started to walk toward the players at second base. As I made my journey to the boys, I heard comments from the stands.

"Come on, ump, make a call. Really? You're going to talk to the kids."

"Come on, blue! Do you really think these kids are going to be honest with you?"

"Yeah, right! Like you can really trust what they're going to tell you!"

When I reached the boys, I asked the runner his name.

"Frank," he replied.

I then asked the fielder.

"Justin," he replied.

"Frank and Justin, can you believe these adults? They're already claiming you'll lie and be dishonest. Would you guys mind helping me prove them wrong?" I asked, pointing to each of their hearts.

"Sure," they both replied.

"That's awesome, guys. I want to be sure we get this call correct. Frank, did you feel Justin tag you before the base?"

"Yes, Sir," Frank said. "I felt his glove on my shoulder." Frank pointed to his right shoulder.

"Hey Justin, did you tag Frank? Do you mind showing me how you tagged him?"

"I did it like this," Justin said, with his hand over the ball and in his glove. "I tagged him on the shoulder."

"Boys, I am very proud of you. I appreciate your both being honest—even when some adults thought you would lie."

Immediately after the game and prior to the teams shaking hands, I called Frank and Justin to the front of the lines at home plate. I addressed the field.

"Ladies and gentlemen, you all saw the play where I was talking to Frank and Justin here. Both of these boys were honest—when many of you thought they would lie. Because Frank and Justin displayed great integrity, I am giving each of them a game ball. Gentlemen, thank you and enjoy your tournament."

As I walked off the field, one parent approached me, holding his head down in shame, and said, "I think you taught us all a lesson today! Thank you!"

Fifth Inning Stretch

Umpire Brian Altenbach

Your character is more important than how good you are at any sport. Athleticism is temporary. Your character, the type of person you are, lasts forever. Be compassionate, be grateful, be humble, be honest.

Bottom of the Fifth: Ball on the Dresser (Honesty in Life)

One day, because I had a free moment to rest and relax, I sat on a bench at a local mall for some people-watching and to enjoy a milkshake. As I sat lost in thought, a young man sat down next to me. After a time, I felt him staring at me. As I turned to look his way, I noticed his fixed look turn to surprise.

"I told my parents it was you," he exclaimed.

With a confused look, I asked, "So I take it that you know me from somewhere?"

"It's me, Justin!" he said excitedly. "From the tournament in the township."

I sat staring for a time, trying to recall him. It finally hit me, "Ahhh, Justin, the tag at second. I asked you and the other player to help me prove the adults wrong by being honest with me. That was many years ago. I'm shocked you remembered me."

"Yep, that was me," he said. "That was a fun day, and I liked that you gave us both a game ball for being honest."

"I'm glad that I was able to do that for you," I said. "I always felt that baseball should be a gentleman's sport and that we need to have integrity as we play. I liked how we proved those adults in the stands wrong."

We sat and spoke a little more about our different baseball experiences, school, his achievements, and general life events. As the discussion went on, Justin said he wanted to share something with me.

"Sure," I said. "I'd love to hear it."

He explained that just about a week ago, his parents told him they needed to talk. They entered his bedroom, and his mom pulled a cigarette pack from behind her back. He immediately knew they had found it in his backpack, as he felt panic and sick to his stomach. A story was developing in his head as he sat on the edge of his bed, staring at the floor with his head in his hands. The thought of telling his parents he was holding them for a friend raced through his mind. He slowly lifted his head.

But then he saw a baseball on his dresser behind his parents. He stared at that ball for what seemed like hours. When he finally looked his parents in the eyes, he felt compelled to tell them the truth.

"You know, blue," Justin said, "I was prepared to lie until I saw that baseball. That was the ball you gave me that day you asked me to help prove those parents wrong. I remembered what you said about the importance of being honest when you gave us the balls."

"What did your parents do?" I asked.

"They said they were surprised I was honest," Justin said.

"How did you feel when you told the truth?" I asked.

"I felt very relieved, and I realized that the person I most needed to be honest with was myself. When I caught sight of the baseball and remembered our conversation, I knew that being honest with myself and my parents was the only thing to do."

"Justin, I'm glad that you were able to be honest with yourself and your parents. I'm glad that our little interaction was a great memory for you. I hope you keep this in mind as you start meeting tougher challenges in life. Thank you for sharing."

We shook hands as we stood to depart. I encouraged Justin to continue on this path and mentioned that honesty is important in all aspects of his life.

As I started to walk away, Justin called, "Hey, blue?"

I turned with a smile, "Yes, Justin?"

With his left hand pointing to me and his right hand over his heart, Justin said, "Stay true!"

Photograph by Nicole Keith

Russell Reimer Field: Mount Bethel, Pennsylvania

The Sixth Inning: Faith

faith

/fāTH/ • *noun*

Confidence and trust in another or a thing

The Baseball Scorecard

	Notes:					Start Time:			Attendance:					
☐	Visitor:			Date:		End Time:			Wind:					
☐	Home:			Scorer:		Time of Game:			Weather:					

#	Line Up	Pos	1	2	3	4	5	6	7	8	9	10	AB	R	H	RBI

S U M S							
	Runs						
	Hits						
	Errors						
	Left on Base						

#	Pitchers	W/L/S	IP	H	R	ER	BB	SO	HB	BK	WP	TBF

#	Catchers	PB		Umpires	
				HP:	3B:
				1B:	
				2B:	

Top of the Sixth: Throwing a Fit (Faith on the Field)

The fall baseball season had finally come upon the area. Games during this season tend to be more relaxed and instructional. Players are moving up in leagues as they gain more experience with a different set of rules. Coaches and umpires work with the players to educate them more about the game.

During one game, a pitcher was having difficulty with different plays in the field. He would flail his arms, stomp his feet, or kick up dirt when frustrated with his teammates. After one play, he did all three, plus threw his glove on the ground with tears in his eyes.

I called time-out and walked out to him.

"Hey, Son. It's okay. What's your name?"

"Keith," he said tearfully.

"Well, Keith," I said, pointing to his heart, "I can tell you care a lot about doing well. I can also tell you panic when other players make plays. I see how your teammates look up to you. It's important for you to have faith in them, to trust they can make plays and get the outs. Believe deep inside yourself, trust deep inside yourself that you and your team can and will work well together. When you do this, you'll notice a difference in how you play."

Keith wiped his tears and was able to get back to pitching. The game proceeded, and I noticed a difference in their play. Keith and his team fought back. He was now encouraging and clapping for them as they made their plays. If a mistake was made, he yelled, "That's okay. Get the next one."

I could see the change in the team, but despite it, they still lost the game by two.

After the game, I met up with Keith and said, "Hey, you and the team fought back. Great job pulling together. I think your encouragement really helped. True character is when you maintain faith—especially when you're being challenged."

"Thank you, blue," he said with a huge smile on his face. "I did start believing and trusting myself and the team. I'll keep working on it."

Bottom of the Sixth: Grandfather (Faith in Life)

Years later, around the holidays, I was out shopping for gifts. As I was looking in a store, I felt a tap on my shoulder and heard a voice ask, "Hey, blue, is that you? You're the speech ump, aren't you?"

I turned to look in the direction of the tap and the voice to see a young man standing with his parents. "It's me. How are you doing? Please forgive me: You look familiar, but I'm having difficulty recalling where from."

"It's me, Keith," he said. "The one you spoke to about faith."

Surprised, I said, "Ah, Keith! Yes, I remember that game. It's been a few years. You look good. Have you still been playing ball?"

Keith indicated he was doing well and still playing. His parents then shook my hand. They stated that they wanted to thank me for the conversation with their son and to inform me the interaction had an impact on Keith. They all asked if I had time for them to share a story.

"Absolutely, I will be glad to hear it," I said.

"At the game where you encouraged me to have faith in my teammates, my grandfather was there," Keith began. "He was finally able to make it to a game, and I was trying to do a great job for him. I was upset that it wasn't going the way I wanted it to go."

Keith's parents shared that it was the first game his grandfather was able to attend and watch as he was having some health difficulties. After the game, his grandfather asked Keith about the conversation the umpire had with him. He shared that he was encouraged to have faith and believe in himself and others.

A small tear came to Keith's eye as he recalled his grandfather telling him that faith is important in everything you do and noting that faith will be important when he is unable to be around anymore. His grandfather shared that the love, faith, and belief he has in him will always be in his heart as his grandfather pointed and touched Keith's heart. His grandfather then hugged him and shared how proud he was of the game he played. The family reported that his grandfather died a month after that game. Condolences were shared.

Then Keith said, "During a science test in school a year after my grandfather had died, I was getting very agitated and upset, trying to answer the questions. My chest was tight. I was breathing heavy, and I wanted to scream and give up. At that moment, I started to think of my grandfather, which brought me back to that game. I heard my grandfather's voice. I felt his hug and a tingly feeling in my heart as I took a deep breath. I told myself that I needed to believe in myself and trust in my abilities. I felt a calm and peace come over me as I completed the exam and earned a B."

As I thanked Keith for sharing, I tapped my finger on his heart and said, "Your belief, faith, and memories of your grandfather will always be inside of you."

The family thanked me for the time and for allowing Keith to share this experience. We exchanged holiday greetings and shook hands.

After I took about six steps away from the family, Keith yelled, "Hey, blue!"

"What's up, Keith?" I asked as I turned to look at him.

With a huge smile on his face and his right hand tapping his heart, Keith said, "Keep the faith!"

The Post-Game: Honor the Diamond

Baseball brings about many emotions, ranging from joy to disappointment. Players work both as individuals and as a team, giving their best efforts to build on successes, limit mistakes, and win the game. We practice to work through game situations and to build upon both individual and team skills. The true test of the individual and team occurs when we are faced with mistakes. Every pitch in every game allows every player a chance to improve and become the best player he can be.

Life is the same. Courage, compassion, gratitude, humbleness, honesty, and faith are key character traits to develop during life. You will learn and develop many more over the years.

In life, your practice is your daily interactions. Just as you have coaches to guide you on the baseball field, your parents, teachers, friends, and family guide you in life. Whether in baseball or in life, the work to be the better player—the better person—comes from inside of you.

As the season comes to a close and I walk off the field toward my car, I turn around and smile in amazement of what occurs on the baseball field. Once I reach my car, I think about that childhood umpire who stood out to me, Cobby. I relive the excitement and joy that I experienced whenever he umpired a game. He was a gentleman with a kind heart, love for the game, and words of encouragement for players. A larger, more content smile emerges as I appreciate how much Cobby's character impacted me.

I return my umpiring gear to its bag and rehang my uniform until next season. I feel at peace as another season ends, allowing me to share in the pride of new lessons learned and experienced by many. Whether on the baseball field or in day-to-day life, personal growth starts when you Honor the Diamond.

Acknowledgments

First and foremost, I need to take this time and extend my deepest gratitude for the life and guidance given to me by my parents, Pat and Paul Altenbach. Their ability to maintain their character in the face of many challenges has demonstrated to me a great deal of integrity that I wanted to pass along to my own children and to others.

I would also like to show my appreciation to both of my boys. I am grateful for my eldest son, Bryton Altenbach, for his candor and forthrightness about his views and ideas about the book when I shared it with him. His suggestions helped me be more focused on some details to make the flow of the book easier to follow. I also appreciate my youngest son, Tristan Altenbach, for his artistic talents and ideas to conceptualize the cover design.

I would also like to extend my thankfulness to Pastor Larry Burd for his words of wisdom and encouragement along my journey of writing. He has a knack for finding the right passage and words to help foster the commitment and trust to my internal understanding to write what needed to be said.

Finally, there isn't enough thanks I can give my wife, Liz Altenbach, for the amount of support and understanding for this passion of mine called baseball and umpiring. When there was a conflict to see our grandchildren and a tournament, I passed along how kids were asking if I was going to be umpiring the tournament. Without hesitation, she stated, "You know you need to do the tournament." It is this unwavering support that is truly amazing. She has been steadfast in her encouragement for me to continue with the desire to complete my book.

About the Author

Brian Altenbach was born and raised in Easton, Pennsylvania, and he has been around baseball his entire life as a spectator, player, coach, and umpire. He is married a second time and has two wonderful boys, a stepdaughter, stepson, and two grandchildren at this time. He is currently a Licensed Professional Counselor who works part-time in private practice counseling individuals through many aspects of life. He works full-time in a local county correctional facility, counseling adults faced with a wide array of charges. As a way to relax from his career, he decided to become a Pennsylvania Interscholastic Athletic Association Baseball Umpire for high school. He is also a member of the National Umpire Association and umpires in the Cal Ripken League of the Lehigh Valley. His collective experiences as a son, father, counselor, and umpire have led him to the formulation of this book.

One of the first memories Brian has as an umpire came when he was about sixteen years old. He was watching his younger brother play a game when adults from another field were asking for a volunteer to umpire a game because the assigned umpire never showed up. The ironic part of this opportunity was that the traditional title of being called "blue" was a real challenge because Brian was dressed all in red. Another fun part of this game was when the coach was refusing to put the team back on the field. He took this opportunity to tell the coach if he failed to field the team it would result in a forfeit. The coach did try to refuse when Brian told the coach he has three seconds to field the team. Parents from both teams thanked Brian for his job and how he handled the situation.

Brian has aspirations to work toward the opportunity to umpire at the Little League World Series. Whether he is able to or not, he plans to umpire as long as possible and to continue to enjoy his interactions with the families and players as they develop themselves. Additionally, Brian will have the time to pass on the passion and love of the game along to his grandchildren. Brian is a firm believer that true change starts from within the person and that the greatest legacy for anyone is their character.